STEALING THE CHILDREN
by
Carolyne Wright

Ahsahta Press

Boise State University
Boise, Idaho

Some of these poems have appeared in:

American Poetry Review, Cutbank, Fathers and Daughters (ed. Lyn Lifshin), *Fragments, Hollin's Critic, Inlet, Intro #9* (ed. George Garrett), *Light, Malahat Review, Pacific, Poetry Northwest, Poets On, Porch, Puget Sound Quarterly, Quarry, Syracuse Poems 1975, Syracuse Poems and Stories 1977, Syracuse Review, Three Rivers Poetry Journal, Waterfront Review,* and *Writer's Forum #5.*

"The Cosmic Scholar" reprinted by permission from *The Christian Science Monitor* © 1977 The Christian Science Publishing Society. All rights reserved.

Poems selected and edited by Dale K. Boyer

Second Printing

ISBN 0-916272-09-5

Library of Congress Catalog Card Number:
78-60226

For my family,
but especially for Marian

Contents

I.   The Cosmic Scholar

II.   Stealing the Children

Note: A centered asterisk at the foot of a page of poetry indicates that the poem continues without stanza division onto the next page.

Introduction

Stealing the Children is Carolyne Wright's first published book of poems. It will, one can predict with confidence, quickly be followed by others. For one of the most arresting and most cheering qualities of these poems is the sense they impart of the fecundity of the imagination from which they derive. Energetic themselves, they intimate reservoirs of energy still untapped. Let me hastily add that there is here no impression at all of resources husbanded, of any kind of parsimonious hoarding. Quite the contrary, it is Ms. Wright's liberality, her sometimes wanton extravagance, that bespeaks an easy and unusual access to experiences from which poems can be made. The liberality, moreover, and the wantonness—a spendthrift indifference to economies with image and metaphor—contribute a special charm to the poems and by establishing the right tone serve their themes.

The lively and varied interests and the sharp, informing eye are the indispensable equipment and also the essential definition of the traveller, and in her book Carolyne Wright appears most often and most character- istically in that generic role. Climbing as if from a sense of duty to herself to "the view you've got to get to," treading "tide flats by night" so that "phos- phorescent algae flare and bloom/ beneath the pressure of my boots," "driving through towns whose names/ claw at the hasps of the throat," or growing "each night, to be the tenured scholar/ of all galaxies," she is almost continuously in exploratory motion, seeing something that wasn't within sight a moment earlier, alerted at every bend in the trail to a discon- tinuity. In the concluding poem, called "Prayer," Ms. Wright alludes to occasional conflict, a choice sometimes to be made, between love and her art ("what's jammed in the typewriter/ or roughed out on the drawing board"), but to this reader such conflict seems less significant, more acci- dental, than their interdependence. Eros is not always showily erotic. It manifests itself in, it is at the root of, the concentrated attention—to things as much as people—that at its best Carolyne Wright's poetry strikingly exhibits.

The landscapes through which the traveller journeys are rendered with the kind of highly selective particularity enabled by knowledge, the fruit of attention. Being wide-eyed, open to wonder, likely to let the pancakes burn in the presence of a volcanic peak that simultaneously stretches upward into blue sky and downward into blue mountain lake—this, we perceive, need not be the sort of naivete that settles for undiscriminating enthusiasms and vague impressions. Ms. Wright is, among other things, a trustworthy naturalist, whose language of description, even when it is most figurative, has the ring and weight of fact.

Nonetheless, these landscapes and the extraordinary sense of physical space, dimensioned and palpably finite, that they cause to be experienced are not the primary subjects of the poems, though they are by no means separable from the primary subjects and not to be slighted. The great divides and rickety trestle bridges to be crossed, the foggy marshes to be groped through, exist, one feels perfectly sure, but they also figure situations in which gestures of the mind and elections of feelings are demanded. They map and re-map the inner life of ongoing relations with others and with oneself. External space, always variable in scale, even within a single poem, can shrink to or dissolve into interior space. Or the two territories may overlay one another, creating an effect of graphic palimpsest, of double, interfused realities: an effect likely to recall, in a creditable, wholly legitimate way, the innovative vision of Theodore Roethke.

So, drowsy in her windswept room, one speaker abruptly becomes "the light of a ship/ navigating in the dark straits of my blood"; and in "Heart's Journey," literal distance, represented in a variety of ways, many of them metaphoric, turns imperceptibly ("There's a place out there/ I've got to get to"—which recalls the already cited "view you've got to get to" from another poem) into disjunctions between two people that neither good will nor ardor can satisfactorily resolve. Examples could be multiplied. Suffice it to say that the author knows what she is up to, knows enough about her technique of blurring the realities to make a joke of it. "Before the moon/ comes up double through the plate glass," she says in "Lines Left from Freedom," "we'll be where we ought to, no matter/ what we call the state—Montana/ Idaho, or disarray—we're in."

Despite the steady reliance on the first and second persons and the impression conveyed that these "I's," "we's," and "you's" refer to people who have an actual existence, there is nothing confessional, nor even particularly autobiographical, about the poems. The characters, unlike the scenery they move through, do not get severally scrutinized, are not individuated, and often seem to blur into one another. Such presence as they have is given by allusion, as if further identification would compromise or falsify their reality for the speaker of the poem, herself scarcely adumbrated. The important reason, however, for a method and effect which, whatever their dangers, are patently deliberated, is that Ms. Wright's overriding concern is almost never with individual people but with relationships: their large and small mutations, their surprises, their limits, their demands, the unrehearsed stances they impose. These subjects— and the list is far from exhaustive, is capable of indefinite extension—gain in impersonal significance because of what Ms. Wright is willing to leave out: portraiture, personality, anecdote, chronological context. They gain even more from what she puts in: the dense imagery of place and move- ment, both external and internal, which pictorializes what would otherwise be intangible, if not abstract, which makes her perceptions into situations and gives them dramatic substance. In other words, she does not report the episodes that have engrossed her; she reimagines them in such terms as isolate from a possible array of interests the stress and strain of human nexus. So in "Taking Leave of Friends" it does not matter what friends the speaker is taking leave of, though it matters very much that they are friends. Nor does it matter who the speaker is; indeed, quite early in the poem she begins to think of herself, address herself, as "you," created by the situation from which she gets all her present relevant meaning.

> You forget time here, forget rhyme, reasons
> for coming, half your name. Who could ask
> where you're going, who would you change
> your life for, whether you'd put a bookmark
> in your heart and rise and follow?

What matters is the experience of a parting from friends, a singular event and also a type of event, the importance of which it is finally impossible to measure. Again and again, as in this poem, Carolyne Wright discerns and defines the essential in such disruptions of relation, such discontinuities, however minor, in the quality and flow of our lives. There is much knowledge in this first book of poems and much reason to look forward expectantly to the books by Ms. Wright that will follow.

Donald A. Dike
Syracuse University
June, 1978

Carolyne Wright is currently an Instructor of English and Creative Writing at Syracuse University, where she completed a Doctor of Arts degree in May, 1979. She was born in Bellingham, Washington, grew up in Seattle, and received her B.A. in English at Seattle University in 1970. A Fulbright-Hayes grant took her to Santiago, Chile in 1971-72, where she studied and translated Latin American poetry, attended art school, and travelled extensively throughout South America. After completing an M.A. in Creative Writing at Syracuse in 1975, she was for six months a novice and then a sister in the Holy Order of MANS. She worked for a time at the University of Washington as a graphic illustrator, and returned to Syracuse for doctoral studies and teaching in 1976. The following year, 1977, Syracuse University awarded her the Academy of American Poets Prize, and in 1979, she received a Breadloaf Scholarship and a residency at Yaddo. In addition to her own poetry, she has published translations of Latin American poetry in many journals, and has exhibited drawings and prints in galleries in both Seattle and Syracuse.

I. The Cosmic Scholar

The Cosmic Scholar

Secretary to the thoughts of others,
I grow, each night, to be the tenured scholar
of all galaxies. I gaze out
at the ancient history of stars—lights,
years old and centuries apart.
Anywhere we are, my text tells me,
is the center of a universe
on the exhale. Stars hurtle out
from every other star, like trees felled
by a meteor. They speed up
as they go—locomotives on an incline
or small boys sneaking out of school to fish.
If we caught up, the novas we've chased
would be old suns, ulcered with spots. . . .
By now I'm lost: the Horsehead Nebula's nostrils quiver;
I race Ferraris 'round the planet's rings.
Before sleep, I shift down-spectrum—
blue to gold to red—and gather, soberly,
my scattered notes. Assembling once again
a face, like a chart of the periodic
elements, I leave it for the morning—
the ditto sheets and cold white stares—
and follow the receding pulsars of the heart,
the stellar vapors reeling as I go. . . .

Ocean Moonset

Third Beach, Washington

I
It's the season to haul in
the run of dreams.

On tide flats by night,
phosphorescent algae flare and bloom
beneath the pressure of my boots.
In the brackish cover in the lee
of dunes, fall-logs crumble.
When the old winds died,
fungus that blooms
in the rings of growing
blew them down. The firm roots
of saplings grip them now.

I try to hold my own ground down;
it shifts and glows with the pressure
of new roots, a different soil.

II
To know time by the moon,
I hike down clockless.
The sky is wide-open as an eye.
If the winds change,
I run through underbrush
to flee fog sliding in.
Always the flight is easier
than standing under fog—
the chill, the hanging moss,
the hours that lose their grip.

III
The kind of horizon—sea or land—

*

the full moon sets behind
when it hauls the tide out,
makes a difference to my ocean.
It has to slip toward midnight
at the world's edge
on its own reflection,
or it's some other country's truth.

IV
Tide runoff flees
like fluttering sandpipers,
then slow, stately gulls.
When it meets the first roll
of fog, it lowers its crest
and glides under.
                  My rising shudder
meets the first undertow
and stills.

V
The Pacific calms me
more than a monastery garden
or Buddha under rain-hung leaves.
Through the fog-muffled roar
of surf, I find my way
toward sleep. Distant breakers
multiply the moon's eye.

VI
My dreams start out
slowly—thin canoes
gliding away from the silhouettes
of hemlocks through the fog.
Shadowy as the thoughts of birds,
they slip toward the darkened
waters of the moon,
the lunar fluid glowing in them
as they go. . . .

The Discipline of Becoming Invisible

The discipline of becoming invisible
is not what you think it is.
Start by driving all night
cross-country, avoiding towns.
Travel light; take breath,
words enough for a few poems,
your clearest sight.
Don't calculate the miles
or wonder if you'll ever get to the point
on the map where your road
breaks off.
        You can't miss invisibility;
it wears your face
inside out. It stares back at you
everywhere:
        It's on the signs at midnight
glowing off the shoulder of the road.
It's in the number of hours
and the sleep it takes
to drain a city out of you.
It's in the light that fires
your retinas with sight.

When you arrive at the tollgate
where the road ends,
you'll pay the last of yourself
out, as the roped nerves
uncoil themselves
from the base of your brain.
Invisibility will be your change;
you'll realize you've carried it
all the way, like chromosomes
or the life maps on your palms.

Now, when you peer into the rear-
•

view mirror, only the road
winds backward in the glass distance.
As you slide away—into the high,
clairvoyant blue of dusk—
you'll wonder what sign it was,
in what unknown code at the road's edge,
first glowed in your sleep
and pointed here,
                where your breath lets go,
and your sight opens
as it turns to light.

Woman in a Greenhouse

I.   She Introduces Herself

I'm a nun in bopper's habit.
I've put away my spectacles
so nobody will recognize me.
They'd be afraid as I am
of the vows that gape wide open
behind my eyes.
                          Don't be astonished.
I'm about as noble as a medieval princess,
renouncing what the scales and the armor
tilted her out of, knocking her back
up against a convent wall.
I can show the secret
I hold between my knees
to no one.

II.   Photograph

A camera squares me off.
I kneel among potted plants
on a greenhouse shelf.
Sun blearing through the smudged glass walls
pushes my face away from them.
Their long leaves tremble too much
when wind bashes against the glass.

My hair is powdered prematurely gray
for the play I must act out
of my system. Dressed up now
like a Bride of Christ
in black wool weeds, I grip
a samurai warrior's sword
until the lace on my cuffs
turns yellow with the effort.
                    *

The photographer says I must see
banners toppling over on a sacred battlefield.
When I turn the blade to my throat,
the glimmer of steel in my eye
sharpens the play to a keen edge. . . .

I haven't got the nerve for such a calling;
my heart is too much an animal
pacing its cage.
But it's an herbivore;
it can't touch raw meat
or feed outside where bare trees
bend double in the wind.
My veins would turn green if it struggled,
and the budding palm shoots
would drop aphids on my wrists.
The sun presses all its weight
against the glass.
If I could only look it in the face. . . .

But I tell my heart, "Secret animal,
there's no way out.
There's only you to bleed through every vein
in my system, before you give us peace.
Then you'll lie among palms in the parlor sun
with me—a woman turned nun
by her own unfurling."

Nun's Song to a Brother

What do I know of him I love?
That's the question I pound
my skull walls with.
I can't beat any bushes flat
trying to get at him.
There are always prayers to say,
or altar cloths to iron,
or the bread to take out of the oven.
There's nowhere to go off alone.
He's caught up, too, and fears the line
and sinker of it. He glares hard
at me between the chapel and the kitchen,
blowfish on the inhale.
My body staves in then, my ribs
the slats of some smelt scow,
stinking with scales. It's then I'd yell
"What's damned's not in the breath
along the neck, the touch;
what's damned is wanting it so much!"
But there's the bell—another class,
another caller, another Mass
to cense the chapel for.
He hurries to the door, smoothing
his impatience down as if it were his hair.
Alone a moment—in one of those silences
we often ward off with our furtive hugs—
I kneel in the pantry like a shrine.
In the dark, before the flap of sandals
calls me back, I've got to loosen
all the cords I've tied for love.

Verge of the Perfect

A late wind rumples the afternoon,
thick with cicadas and sun. In my room,
sleep's arms take me in;
one thought lowers my eyelids,
draws me down. . . .
                  I'm the light of a ship
navigating in the dark straits
of my blood, where clappers clang
on tin, and whirlpools gurgle and suck hard
in the water, and the weighed anchor
pulls my ropes in and in and in. . . .

A green chill lays hands on my skin.
It's as if the mind, oversleeping
by habit, tosses the covers back
and sits up fast: What is the thing,
thin as breath, I've been trying
to catch hold of all these deaths?
I know its hum—a million crickets
scissoring; it rubs through thought's
casing, breaks the will's wings off.
It's a gray water, a bomb buried
in a field, verge of the Perfect
where my skin dissolves. . . .

Insomnia and Its Meters

It's all habit, insomnia and its meters,
ground down each dawn like a knife
on a whetstone. I pace it, each heart-
beat and each word, like an animal
adapting itself to its cage.
The mind hammers its anvil then,
clatters its cutlery against the bars:
What about the hours that go slack
alone? The thoughts that pick their pimples
when nobody's watching? What can I do
to bribe the four walls of the room?
On a scrap of newsprint, in a crack
under the rug, I've scrawled out and stuck
the truth: My soul's a strive-by-nighter
jolted from its seat by a fiercer worker—
the dawn sun splattering on the smudged glass
like the hot suds flung by the housecleaners.
The world's too full of windows
for us, late-shifters, plugging away at sleep
like damaged piecework, wrestling with our pillows
as if they were angels—until the lumpy things
sprout wings, and bless us with safe coverings
from the bright fists shaking at us in our dreams.

Heart's Journey

for J.

How close you are: a small voice
through the Transatlantic cable,
the lights of a city glowing
on night clouds,
a planet shrunk to a fly-speck
at the wrong end of a telescope.
A mountain range away,
clouds begin the long gallop into storm.
The trees, arched bridges
tremble on the ponds. The wind
flaps open—its most decrepit wing.
There's a place out there
I've got to get to;
would you keep one light on,
one door open to admit my thoughts?
What I'll bring: bird's throats
for your silence, one flower
to meet the solitude.

Spokane Reservation School Teacher: Welpinit, Washington

They used to have a dentist all day
Thursday. Now, you wait three months
or hitch to Spokane when the root's ache
breaks your stoicism down. Sharp operators
still cut Indians open at the B.I.A.
They do it to each other at the bars.
To live here, stay on automatic, keep
emergency systems on all night,
miss your lover only once a week.
When the bookmobile wheels in, hide there,
read how missionaries staked conversion
claims on tribes, worried at each others'
like tribe terriers over buffalo scraps.
Your school's an old God-trap of theirs,
earthed up now like a sod-sided council lodge.
Teenagers pass furtive peace pipes
through the fence at recess. If you weren't
the boss, brought from outside like a Jesus book,
you'd join them. Instead, you skirt the rules
like the obscene Salish scribbled
on latrine walls, follow the pretense
of coincidence, catch the savages red-handed.
Alright peace chiefs, back inside.
Finally Friday. You close the grade book
in the late light slanting over empty desks,
catch the last rush hour rattletrap to town.
Your lover got the letter, thought it over,
lounges for you by the baggage counter.
All weekend you try to intersect
with something worth saying.
Sunday evening, it's like your blood's run thin,
your language dying, buffalo gone north.
Nowhere left but the reservation.

*

The whiteman leaves you at the depot;
one quick kiss and he's gone, remote
as a black robe, council fires smoking
on far bluffs, a leaf spinning into the night.
Now you know how they felt.

Drive to Port Townsend

for Sally Harpole

It's so lush, hemlocks crowding to the shoulders
block our view, pencils jostling the words' edges.
Names rush by: Suquamish, Kitsap, Lemolo,
pungent as steam rising in the rain.
Hoods Canal Bridge next, wide as a hungry woman.
Shadows stripe the road with gray going in.
In town, we buy coffee, unpack unwelcome
sack lunches in the Town Tavern and Deli,
watch the bellies of groupies, swelled big
as grocery bags with eight month's weight.
No underwear. Everything gets going
under tie-dyed shifts like pumpkins
waggled at the ends of vines. By the time
we get ours, their first daughters
will be their age, thickening already
at the waist. We wonder did they think twice,
ever fill the room with that man's word
No? The bearded hipsters down their Coors,
clack pool cues on favorite balls,
their women shadows they leave in the booths.
We walk out. The porch, fake puncheons.
Loners, pals, or serial monogamists,
we sink heels in tide flats, trip
earth-shod toes on tap roots, test
once again our code—that one-potato
two-potato road—or gaze what we call
clear-eyed over water gone on so forever
it's like nothing's there at all.

Lake Deveraux Kingdom

Kitsap Peninsula, Washington

We turn the battered inquisitor's eye
on. Night reeds whisper, then pipe down.
Frogs dig green elbows in the ooze,
scrabble toward a getaway
like professors after midterms.
Only the bull toads sit, squat and numinous
as Nubian potentates, belches booming
over the still lake like proclamations,
courtier's palms on drums.
Don't rock the dock, we whisper.
Flick flashlights off. We don't bump
thin-skinned subjects from the kingdoms
of their logs. Let them go, damp coats
spotted and striped as mandrake roots
by wells. We'll wait, watch the star-
crammed sky tremble with portent,
note a bat flit out, on sonar, to meet
armies of insects assembling in dark.
If we doze, warnings will rise and fall
like swells of pondweed, fingering our sleep.
Awake, we'll wait for the lake
to part like a mouth in surprise,
for the stifled boomings of the toad-tribes'
flight, chariots off the highway
clanking after, mud on their wheels
grinding the treads to a halt.

for Linda Edling

Query

I. Query

Falling in love. Is it like falling
in leaves or in battle, answering
some great call—a banner
spattered with gore and holy water?
Can one fall out of it,
the way I fell from my horse while jumping,
the eyes in my stomach wrenched apart?
Or is it another dream, in which, stepping
off sleep's dock, I hurtle down in dark—
an empty skin the force of fall sucks
thinner—till my body breaks
on my bed and I wake?

II.   Invitation to a Response

In this clan, we say, "Love's
the mother cat at the kitten's scruff,
the broom that sweeps the dust-mice up,
the place you set at table
for the tramp out back.
                        Love's got no dimes
hid in a barrel, and wears no powder
on its face, and keeps no Sunday-only schedule.
Love needs no bed
or clean white muslin stained with red."

We warn you: people's edges wear out
here. We pull down the brackets
from around our thoughts.
We're not afraid to be taught
by a hand opening, or be caught
exchanging tongues when the elevator halts.
We trade off voices, share the ins and outs

*

of breath, adopt the drunkard's children. At
our deaths, no cousins finger wallets
or nod long faces through the dull parts
of the sermon.
                    And when we love,
it's not the drop of the prom queen's glove
into the concrete mixer. Our ways
are plain and square-edged
as our tables; our private promises
crawl out of their single beds
at night and join the other fellows';
our children are the fruit of frank loins
and well-oiled elbows.
                    By what other means
can we invite you? Only by this:
some simple gesture—a mere stooping
to pull a tired traveller's
wet boots off—may stop one of you
from jumping, out of love,
out of some late night,
darkened second-storey window.

Dreamers

for J.

We're dreamers of the same dream,
you and I. I keep meeting you knocking
on the front door of my sleep, wondering
what to answer if I said, Come in.
I always say it. You hesitate, reasons
suddenly gone bankrupt as a store,
no business being there. You walk off,
clouds of questions swirling around you
like a cape. It's as if you thought
"Ziggurat," built to infinity, stopped
just short. You'd climb, dear,
but the more inside your fear you are
the harder it is to see it. Your spirit
seethes on the back burner, daring
some angel to stir it. I walk into
the kitchen, spoon in hand.
The strait jacket strains in your face,
unable to conceal how you've watched
for this. I turn to blend the ingredients
of two dreams, wait for the grudging smile
to grow up to joy, for your hands,
waking, to take me by the shoulders,
turn our lives around.

A Choice of Lives

for J., H.O.O.M., Duboce and Steiner, San Francisco

What do you do? No one from your old life
answers when you phone. You don't know
how to put the first lines down
on paper. A bug that crouches
on the table, whittling its antennae,
draws the focus from your memoranda. . . . Ah,
tomorrow: put your finger on the want ad's
perfect job, visit mother in the post-op ward,
forget the one in Omaha, who, when you proposed,
said No. Outside, street cars screech
in protest going around steel curves.
Drunks rant at the corner. Novices
who can't go on with it break down.
In here, you disappear among the lives
in clerics steering quiet down the hall,
ships in a canal, the whole force
of the universe in harness. Chapel:
you can pray till peace refuels you
in its blue flame, you give up
the thoughts that make your mind look
like what's sprawled outside the door.
But there's the bell: another counsel-seeker
maybe, or the head nurse, or the woman
finally arriving from the other end
of your letter. You sigh, each day
the choice of lives repeated like a prayer
you can't live up to. You head toward
the caller at the door, the big move
set aside another hour.

Re-Entry

I have come, ready, this time,
for anything. I've travelled all night
and have little to show for it:
fog that hung in beggar's shreds
from the shoulderblades of the ranges,
bees that flew heavy from flowers,
lost in pollen like a sorrower in grief,
and one thing learned the hard way:
those who prophesy only tunnel
at the end of the tunnel
lead us far from what we left home for,
leave us crying on the old doorsteps,
children who've ridden the nightmare
far too long. Experiences not worth
repeating: scoffers who talk backwards,
thieves who sever each other's dirt-
creased fists, and cross, against the light,
at a stagger.
                    Take me. I'm steadier now,
can let calm hands curve around my heart,
coax out the light whose blaze discloses
what I had no patience for: a world
where nothing comes before we're ready,
where we conquer the cracks in every
dawning thought, our private rituals
take boarders, fold back the sheets,
put away the mirrors. Let the loner's
authority fade from my face, ears
so tuned already to the vows I'll take
I hardly notice where the old voice goes,
begging its questions at the teacher's door.

II.   Stealing the Children

The Right Set of Fears

for Marian

You've tried to choose me the right set
of fears: don't walk alone at night;
don't quit, or settle for defeat;
don't marry the romantic for his brief delights
or bow to the broken image at the end.
Think of common interests, common friends;
think of old age, and heat in winter.
Thank you, mother, but not even Siddhartha,
who starved and prayed for wisdom all his life,
could save his only son from strife.
And I—whose vision still is checked by fear,
even as light slides the membrane
from my eye—should I revere
the advice you followed, that fearful wisdom,
as you age between the laundry and the kitchen,
a wandering husband and my letters home?

Pater Familias

for Donald

The air always filled with the word
No. Weekends, he dozed before the T.V. set,
slouched downstairs to open drawers;
sent up, through the vents, the glass's clink
against the bottle. We were too small
to stand up to dictums issued
from the breakfast throne. Mother's shoulders
rounded under his glare—truncated in love
she was, like a cry cut off. She slipped us
dollar bills, wheedled riding lessons,
concert seats, treats that tried to fill
the holes. Falling asleep, our shoulders
twitched, rejecting everything he said:
whisperings at midnight, audible shrugs,
evasions stumbling down the steps
to face up to just one more round. . . .

                    The red face fades.
The first decades recede like a hairline.
Colleagues tell us we're successes,
come over the landscaped hills of circumstance
to freer pasture: concert grands, podiums
pounded so hard they stand up to poems,
real friends. Down the old street,
mother's still round-shouldered, waits
for phone calls or our letters,
cakes she bakes for our arrivals
getting smaller every year.

Magnolia Bluff

for Paul

Rank on rank of odors climb the bluff,
seaweed that out-stenches spinach,
hangs clammy as rubber gloves from the rocks.
Only tide has any muscle to it.
Here, where ferries plow back and forth
dependable as tractors, your mind
turns like a trick ankle on the cliffs
and drifts down harbor with the wreckage.
Your brothers are successes,
understudy governors, swivel in desk chairs
in the foundry owner's office. Your van's
ramshackle as your pad, the sleeping bag
you doze on oil-stained, your job
the figment of some commissioner's
municipal imagination. You'd like to get
what they got: what they wanted.
Or these consolations: driftwood piles
here for the collecting, you can sight
through the knotholes as if they were sextants,
as if you piloted the ship. Better yet,
planes take off from Sea-Tac everyday
for anywhere you'd like to hide,
or start over, or coming down the ramp,
resume that interrupted flight,
your stride.

Taking Leave of Friends

Lake Union Dock, Seattle

A spot picked at damp random
to break through: the line of docks
spattered with creosote, workmen
hosing down a seaplane on the fritz,
silence in the beam-strewn yards
between warehouses. How will we get out
of this one? you ask the red ant
toppled from a rusted cable to your thigh.
Migrations are the mainstay: a gaggle
of honkers lined up on the shore,
calls hollow with tundra, thawed ice
booming under all-night sun.
Long sad distances unravel
from their bandaged throats.
Strange currents catch the skirts
of your thoughts on the updraft.
You forget time here, forget rhyme, reasons
for coming, half your name. Who could ask
where you're going, who would you change
your life for, whether you'd put a bookmark
in your heart and rise and follow?
Who would know how true you are, no matter
what the year, no matter what the rip tides
of your blood washed in? Clouds
piling up on the horizon show you
who your friends are, love
the outbound bus you climb aboard,
your strongest word goodbye.

Western Trails Cafe

Tremonton, Utah

In the lazy Western cafes,
even flies on the sills
seem to be droning underwater.
Waitresses lounge against the short-
order counter, gape as the busload
comes lumbering in, each group turning
to its booth like steers to the feed stalls.
Hands holding forks move up and down,
a busboy swipes at the table tops,
the postcard rack creaks slowly
as it swings around.

To the south, the world to come continues
with the preparations for its own arrival.
Japanese fruit farmers stoop in the rows
and hoe hard as in Honshu; a lone note
too high for human hearing goes up
from Moroni's trumpet on the Temple top;
and dressed-up families walk toward whatever it is
that they worship, as a flock of gulls
rises, circles, and heads for the Great Lake
in a line as straight as any crow could make.

Heading for Cover:
Great Salt Lake, Utah

The salt flats spread out
like a widening mind.
The moon sits on the water,
a cracked plate on a table.
In patches, the bare skull
of the world shows.
At the lake's edge, we head
for meager cover—junipers
and boulders split down the middle
like heads. Cover us, night.
We must depart in secret.
Still here, still here, the killdeer's
whistle mocks. Everywhere we step,
broken sticks talk back in the dark.

Stealing the Children: After a Big Wind in Wyoming

It's not the kind of country where you can walk
dry-eyed. An olive-green wind blows
dust up and down the alleys,
gathers dry leaves in its fists for storm.
It's the kind of town where,
if you leave your children unattended,
the wind drives up for them
in its long, black station wagon.
They go so willingly they leave their tricycles
scattered over three backyards.
Later, you roam the feedlots,
poking among freight rails that writhed
like wounded serpents while the twister
passed over. Your own mind
is blown so dry it can't recall
who they were, those who left in mid-gale,
clambering into the front seat of the wind,
not even waving goodbye as they blew down
the street, leaving only scraps of their voices,
like strewn toys, on your lawn.

The Trestle Bridge

Cheyenne, Wyoming

Far off, the rumble of freights
through junctions. The moon rides,
aloof and full of herself,
above the cottonwood branches.
In the slough, a beaver pokes its head
through a ripple, slaps its tail,
shatters the moon. Not an echo left
of silver in her trail.
I cross the high train trestle
to the animal shelter at the prairie's edge.
Dogs' eyes stare like inmates'
from the cell blocks. As I walk off,
a wail, claws rake the bars,
chains, like loons' throats, rattle.
On the tracks again, a killdeer shrills
a warning, drags its wing.
I let it fool me from the freight yard nest,
hatchlings in the tufts between oil drums.
Everything's bent on one more breath,
another dive for insects in the evening air,
a branch hacked for fence posts
or a dam. High up, a dark wind starts
in the junipers. My life fits its body,
passenger on the outbound car.

                                                  All I hear,
at the last bridge, by the broken ties,
is that the crossing to the other side is mine.

Flatiron Trail

Boulder, Colorado

It's a precarious viewpoint.
Mainly you climb to where the flatiron
heaves above the pines' crests,
a sinking liner's prow. Moraine
of hot shale sliding underfoot
like stale friends, always on the phone
when you need them. All afternoon,
the yellowhammer's bill batters the bark.
Finally you're above the two-way traffic
on the trail. You can point, say "people,"
an edge of scorn in your voice
as if you weren't. No streams this high,
nowhere to drink like a deer does,
watching the sky in the water.
It's the view you've got to get to.
Not even a gray fox peering around
a boulder with its shyster's face
can trick you off the trail. The view.
You've seen enough adultery in hallways,
breezes down the corridors thickening
like skin, opting for love's reasonable
facsimiles. The sun comes over the rock rim,
stares into the shadow like a jealous god.
You straddle Saddle Rock like an illicit lover.
Take control. Your thoughts have words,
walk upright. Everything under jack pines
pays attention, chameleons doing watchful
pushups on the stone. Unbend your life.
Walk straight down the mountain. Into view.
The gray fox, sentry on the landing,
stares you home.

Boredom, Nevada

for Richard Hugo

A state that's gone white in my mind.
The air's so flat with salt, dust sweats.
You can ride for miles till your horse
dries out. The distant hills blue
as cop cars. Back in Utah, all they've got
's avenging angels—gold Moroni toppling
off the Temple like a safe, stamping out
some life of crime. Gold quarter horses
fill glass cases at the Chevron station;
their flesh counterparts lope out, fresh,
on fence patrol, limp back from Midas,
turned nothing but exhausted.
Bleak towns fill the pages of my book.
I look out the window for relief: bleak towns.
Even my friends' eyes are full of them.
We drive through Mote: "No Services Available."
Not even Sundays. When we hit Remote,
we wonder wait a minute weren't we here before.
At Valmy, the first settler to stagger
through the canyon croaked, "This is the place."
And dropped cold. It's so dead now
not even time passes. Some folks still say,
"Till Kingdom come." Here, Till Boredom goes.
Even the dust's so bored it turns in on itself,
goes twisted through the sagebrush
trying to kick up a storm.

Mt. Mazama Series

I.   The Way to Mt. Mazama

after Han-Shan

Hauling all our garbage and no water,
we've driven since dawn to Crater Lake,
skipping out of last night's camp site
before the ranger came by to collect the fee.
At the first overlook, by the information
sign, we cook breakfast. Tourists
ask us questions as if we were experts.
What we do know: rim volcanoes
plunge into the air as far as mirrored
ones reach down through the water.
With such a view, deeper, clearer
than sky reflected in a roshi's eye,
can we be held accountable
for burning the pancakes?

II.   Crater Lake: a Second Look

By Llao Rock, the sign commands
"DON'T FEED THE BIRDS. Your charity's
their doom. Long-tailed weasels
feast on them in winter; hunger
and diseases take the final toll."
We cram ourselves with pancakes,
wonder what to do with extra batter.
Each hotcake's a reflection of the lake:
bubbles where the craters are, fine lines
where jet contrails slice across the water.
We could take postcard shots, cross
spatulas and bread knives on our breasts
like Ramses, height of his power, graven
on the stone boat coffin, the Lower
Kingdom's image. . . . In China,
they'd wash their ears of such suggestions.
We, in the West, just wash our hands.

III.   Dream on Scott's Mountain

The best poems slipped away like gravel
over Eagle Crag. I climbed from my body
to look for them, found instead a ladder
propped up in a stream, half the rungs
mossy, others gone. Thoughts arrived
from various lovers and all the members
of my family, collected on the bank
like paper boys, waiting for me
to answer or pay up. You slouched
in back, balancing in one hand
the plate of pancakes I'd forgotten,
one sticky finger pointing,
the syrup dripping from the rim.
I clung to the rot-seamed slats;
the stream slid underfoot. Fingerlings
nibbled at my ankles, flicked off
at a kick like tropes whose meanings
are hardly sought for, seldom caught.
Hoots got louder from the bank.
A pole thrust out, prodded
like a fork into a short stack.
I had to climb back up the hard way,
find myself empty, hover over
like a 'copter till the flight director
woke up, called me in.
At the top of the ladder,
the mountain would begin.

IV.   Descent from Mt. Mazama

Guides to these trails tell all
the names, none of the stories:
Sun Notch, where Mt. Mazama lava roared
to Klamath Lake, made marsh grass boil.
Wizard Island, cone thorning
from the pocked cheek of the earth.
Tokotee, where dawn light splashes
glacial on the spruce. We can take
cross sections of ourselves; let old parts
fall away like chunks of glacier
crashing rotten to the lake.
The only stories are the slow grind
of bedrock down the mountain, rain
that scrubs the rock face smooth,
lichen clinging in mendicant's tatters
from the octopus of lava spills.
All deer settle with their cuds at dawn.
Trees draw down oxygen, send back the rain.
Only hocked cars, hot with mileage,
blast through the clear, sub-alpine air,
knocking the souls of trees flat,
rock-and-roll tunes sticking their feet
through the dashboards, kicking
the back-seat drivers.

Sleeping in the Open: Coos Bay, Oregon

The chill gulls call, hunch
in their feathers. Killdeers bunch
and scatter, start the stuttering
of wingbeats south. We're following
the long waist of the coast,
driving through towns whose names
claw at the hasps of the throat:
Siuslaw, Clatsop, Kilchis River.
You drive, while I attend to vital matters:
smoke of campfires ghosting through alders
toward the greater gray of sky,
stump tops of pilings dripping with salal,
low tide slipping like a cover
off the seabed, leaving tide wrinkles
naked, fiddler crabs scuttling for shelter
like brittle women in stiff skirts.
It's late when we steer into the camp lot,
needle veering toward empty, the last gas
ticking out. We pitch your slack tent
in salt-stiffened wind, and sink back
to ourselves, coiled shells closing,
gray whales sounding an unheard-of deep.
We sleep, and dream that night of trawlers
anchored far out, hulls ice-blue
and nameless, nets reeling in and out.
We dream of green hands reaching
toward the nets through fog.
I wake: a shot volleying
across the broad back of the night.
You stir, shift a little. I lie quiet,
ears turned like an animal's to dark.
Dawn, a thought's face coming over us.
Tide slaps on the pilings; in the morning,
we'll see wharves beaten down for years
have backed up, stood all night
between us and the sea.

Lines Left from Freedom

for Julia

East, out of Butte, Kennecott's ore pile
heaps like a streaked, stained skirt:
laundry some dying miner's wife forgot.
Junipers climb foothills out of town,
swarthy, dwarfed as those shepherds
in the Holy Land photos—scrawny goats
blatting about them, swathed women
following, in shadow no matter how high
the noon. The continent divides
at Homestake. One last haul
and we're over—no sweat in this air-
conditioning, driver down-shifting,
a rocking-chair codger's lifetime
from the cracking axletrees
pioneers strained and prayed over.
No doubt in our minds, at 70, on 90,
we'll make it to Billings this evening.
At Big Sky, the driver gets a ticket,
backs off the interstate, takes the old
road through the canyon. Basalt
and switchbacks fill the afternoon.
A hundred-ore-car freight crawls past:
four engines. Derelict switching sheds
crumble every junction. We sigh
and fan ourselves in the dry cold sweat,
patient heroines, not so worked-up-
and-at-'em we forget to grin.
With billboards to read, and signs
for those who see deer on roadways,
and rye grass that blows up, throwing
its seeds out at the nearest wind,
why should we push it? Before the moon
comes up double in the plate glass,

*

we'll be where we ought to, no matter
what we call the state—Montana,
Idaho, or disarray—we're in:
following the Yellowstone toward morning,
the long way into town.

Otisco Road

with thanks to Inez and Henry

Evening on the increase. Dark drops
before our eyes where we expected light.
Mist rises from the pastures, fields
stripped of corn, wrecked stalks
plowed under. The wind's throat is hollow
as a distant owl's with fall.
You've welcomed me here, to a resting place
at the end of my thoughts. Not that we have
the final say on life. All the returns
aren't in yet; most of our past
is out of reach. I put myself in your hands,
friends, knowing we'll make it into town
on time. The rest is easy: straightening up
the storeroom when what's stored there
piles high and topples; keeping a finger
on the pulsing of our thoughts;
running the sheep and goats together,
pelt by pelt. No openings in town
for worry. If the sun were out now
we'd be tall as the field is long.
It's not, but we're warm, and can still
make out the maple that flames
from the sudden dusk of the yard
like a banner gone before us.
Let's go in. Dinner's on, and rust
or thieves will have the car and combine
if they want them: all the big machinery
we have to leave out in the rain.

Prayer

for Stephen

Bless my life—its inks
and paperweights and houseplants
fringed with sun.
Give me the quiet, Lord,
I close my eyes
and turn my tongue back for.
Don't feed me too much,
and when I can't decide between love
and what's jammed in the typewriter
or roughed out on the drawingboard,
take away the coins I flip
and make me listen: That young man
smiling in my kitchen at me is in love.
With me. That's one door in my house
that opens on more than grief
or dirty sheets or the supermarket
twice a week. It gives on light,
and I, your moth, am beating to get in.
Give us this day, and with no promises
but what we are—two small people
trying to be one—send us out
and say, "That's fine. Light fills your gaps.
Breathe on."

Ahsahta Press

MODERN AND CONTEMPORARY POETRY OF THE WEST

1975-76 (Modern series)

Selected Poems, by Norman Macleod
Selected Poems, by Gwendolen Haste
New & Selected Poems, by Peggy Pond Church

1976-77 (Contemporary series)

A Taste of the Knife, by Marnie Walsh
Headlands, Rising, by Robert Krieger
Winter Constellations, by Richard Blessing

1977-78 (Modern series)

My Seasons, by Haniel Long
Selected Poems, by H. L. Davis
Women Poets of the West: An Anthology

1978-79 (Contemporary series)

Stealing the Children, by Carolyne Wright
Songs, by Charley John Greasybear
Over DeSoto's Bones, by Conger Beasley, Jr.

1979-80 (Modern series)

The Hearkening Eye, by Hildegarde Flanner
To the Natural World, by Genevieve Taggard

i